To the Austin Family,

Thank you for your hospitality and friendship throughout my stay in America

Your Aussie
Andrea.

W9-DHS-828

PRO HART'S
Waltzing Matilda

National Library of Australia
Cataloguing-in-Publication entry

Hart, Pro, 1928–
    Pro Hart's Waltzing Matilda.
    ISBN 0 7270 1167 7
    1. Hart, Pro. 1928–. 2. Paterson, Andrew Barton,
    1864–1941. Waltzing Matilda—Pictorial works.
    3. Paintings, Australia. I. Jenkin, Graham Keith,
    1938–. II. Paterson, Andrew Barton, 1864–1941.
    Waltzing Matilda. III. Title.

759.9'94

RIGBY LIMITED • ADELAIDE • SYDNEY
MELBOURNE • BRISBANE
First published 1979
Reprinted 1980
Copyright © 1979 Kevin C. Hart
All rights reserved
Wholly designed and typeset in Australia
Printed in Hong Kong

PRO HART'S
Waltzing Matilda

with an Introduction by
GRAHAM JENKIN

RIGBY

WALTZING MATILDA

Oh! there once was a swagman camped in the Billabong,
Under the shade of a Coolabah tree;
And he sang as he looked at his old billy boiling,
'Who'll come a-waltzing Matilda with me.'

Who'll come a-waltzing Matilda, my darling,
Who'll come a-waltzing Matilda with me?
Waltzing Matilda and leading a water-bag—
Who'll come a-waltzing Matilda with me?

Down came a jumbuck to drink at the water-hole,
Up jumped the swagman and grabbed him in glee;
And he sang as he put him away in his tucker-bag,
'You'll come a-waltzing Matilda with me!'

Down came the Squatter a-riding his thoroughbred;
Down came Policemen—one, two, and three.
'Whose is the jumbuck you've got in your tucker-bag?
You'll come a-waltzing Matilda with me.'

But the swagman, he up and he jumped in the water-hole,
Drowning himself by the Coolabah tree;
And his ghost may be heard as it sings in the Billabong,
'Who'll come a-waltzing Matilda with me?'

A. B. *Paterson*, Saltbush
Bill, J.P. and Other Verses,
1917.

The words of 'Waltzing Matilda' have been reproduced by permission
of the copyright owner.

'Waltzing Matilda' is *not* Australia's official national anthem, and it is not likely that it will be in the foreseeable future. But, without doubt, if there is a song by which Australia is internationally recognised, then it is this stirring bush song which was conceived on Dagworth Station early in 1895. And it is 'Waltzing Matilda', above all other songs, which has the power to moisten the eyes of the Australian abroad—whether he be overseas on business or pleasure, in peace or in war—just as the smell of eucalyptus leaves takes his heart and mind back to the ancient continent of his birth, and calls forth countless memories of that 'kind old land'. And it is 'Waltzing Matilda' which heightens the Australian's awareness of his nationality and reminds him that he is a member of a distinctive nation of people with an exciting and colourful past, and the inheritor of great traditions.

To understand why this should be so, it is necessary for us to consider some of the fascinating history which lies behind this story, and also some of the very interesting history of the song itself.

Perhaps we should start by clarifying the meaning of the term 'waltzing Matilda'. Various theories have been put forward as to the derivation of this term, but there is certainly no argument about its meaning. 'Waltzing Matilda' simply means 'carrying a swag'. There are a number of synonymous terms, the most popular of which include 'humping the bluey' and 'humping the drum'. Bluey, drum, and swag are different names for the same thing, namely a bed-roll; and a bluey-humper or a swagman is simply a man travelling through the bush carrying all his utensils and possessions—including his bed-roll—with him. His utensils vary, but the most important would be his billy, for boiling water to make tea or for cooking stew, dumplings, and so forth; his water bag; and his tucker bag, in which he carried his flour and anything else which he could 'borrow'—such as beef or mutton. Thus, with his swag to sleep in and his billy to cook in, the swagman was able to survive and flourish indefinitely in the bush; and wherever he decided to roll out his swag for the night—then that was home.

The swag is a much bigger thing, far more useful and infinitely more important (culturally and in every other way) than what is nowadays called a sleeping bag. For a start, the swag is usually waterproof. This is achieved by employing waterproof duck or a canvas tent-fly as the outside covering for the swag. So it doesn't matter much whether it's raining or not: once you are in your swag you are warm and dry for the night (unless you've been foolish enough to camp in a swamp).

Another useful aspect of the swag is that it serves as a portable wardrobe. The usual practice adopted by bushmen is to put their spare clothes, plus towel and toiletries, inside a pillow case or bag, and to roll it up inside the swag. This practice also provides them with a comfortable pillow. In fact any small items can be carried in this way, and it is handy to be able to put papers, writing gear, medicine (such as brandy, for snake-bite) all inside the one container, which also happens to be bed and home.

Not the least advantageous of the swag's many roles is that it constitutes an excellent and comfortable seat. Around any campfire in any corner of the continent where stock are being mustered or overlanded as you read this (if it be evening or night) men will be lounging against or sitting happily on their swag, the most distinctively Australian seat of all. They will be watching billies boil on the fire, or lighting pipes or rolling cigarettes and yarning, just as their fathers and their grandfathers and great grandfathers did before them.

For the swag certainly has not fallen into disuse—far from it. In fact, with the introduction of motorised transport, swags have become even more elaborate, and many now include a mattress of one kind or another as well as blankets, swag cover, swag straps, and all the other paraphernalia previously mentioned. An excellent description of the construction and contents of nineteenth century swags is to be found in Henry Lawson's sketch: 'The romance of the swag'. But present-day swag-owners will realise that our national portable bed-cum-wardrobe has changed but little, if at all, during the intervening decades.

It should be pointed out that the ownership of a swag does not necessarily denote a swagman. The number of swagmen alive today must be so small as to be negligible, but there are thousands of swag-owners. And even when 'Waltzing Matilda' was written, and many more people were using swags than there are today, only a certain proportion were described as swagmen.

Most bushmen, no matter what their specialist occupation happened to be—whether stockman, drover, shearer, digger, or any other itinerant vocation—spent much of their sleeping time in swags. But they were only described as swagmen when they were carrying their swags from one station to the next looking for work. So a man might be a shearer this month, a swagman for the next week, then a shearer or station hand for the following month or so. Interestingly enough, the sizeable proportion of bushmen who were mounted when looking for work, and whose swags were carried by packhorses, were not usually designated swagmen.

A final note on this point: there was, among swagmen, a small specialist group called 'sundowners'. These were 'professional' full-time swagmen whose aim in life was simply to go on being swagmen and to avoid work if it could possibly be avoided. They were called sundowners because they generally contrived to arrive at a station at about sundown, when it was not too late to obtain some tucker—flour, tea, sugar, and perhaps a bit of freshly-killed mutton or beef—but it was too late to do any work. They were generally gone by early morning.

It might be asked: why did the squatters and station managers give such men anything at all? The answer is twofold: firstly, it was an old bush tradition and part of the accepted etiquette; and secondly, squatters who failed to honour the tradition tended to find partly consumed sheep at various parts of their runs, or, worse still, they became particularly prone to bush fires. It was said that Bryant and May (the famous match manufacturers) were the swagman's best friend! But it must be stressed that the overwhelming majority of swagmen were not sundowners, and their whole purpose in carrying their swags was to obtain seasonal work, the very nature of which forced them to be nomadic.

The term 'waltzing Matilda' applied to a man carrying a swag appears to have been a regional one, confined originally to an area of central western Queensland. But when the song became popular it was widely adopted, although not, apparently, by the men themselves. There are a number of theories regarding the way in which the swag came to be christened 'Matilda'. While all of them are conjectural, Harry Pearce's theory that it is derived from the German words *walzen* (slang for strolling) and *Mathilde* (nickname for a female companion) seems to be about as likely as any.

According to Pearce, apprentices and journeymen in Austria and Germany referred to their travels as *auf der walz*; while soldiers referred to the greatcoats which they carried (rolled up like swags) as *Metzes* or *Mathildes*. Both of these names were used disparagingly to mean whore or camp follower, and an extension of the terms to refer to the coats and blankets (which often had to take the place of real *Mathildes*) seems to be a natural development. The journeymen, says Pearce, also referred to the bags of tools which they carried as *Mathildes*.

With substantial numbers of German migrants arriving in the continent since the 1830s, the application of the term '*walzen Mathilde*' to the indigenous swagmen also seems perfectly natural, as does its anglicised form, 'waltzing Matilda'. Thus, although there is no real proof to support the argument, it is certainly the most plausible explanation of the many which have been proffered in an attempt to explain the derivation of the term, and one which, at this stage, may safely be accepted.

Other terms in 'Waltzing Matilda' which may need explanation are the following:

billabong: an old branch of a river which water enters only when the river is high. This billabong was dry (apart from its waterhole) at the time the song was written, and it thus made a good camping spot.

coolabah (or coolibah): *Eucalyptus microtheca*, a tree occurring over a wide area of inland Australia. Normally, it is of medium height (about 14 metres) with a wide spread of thin, dull foliage. Like the tree in the song, most coolabahs are to be found along waterways or in areas likely to be flooded.

leading a water bag: in drier country, and in the dry season, it was usually necessary to carry a canvas water bag when travelling on foot. The water bag not only holds a good quantity of water, it also cools it by allowing moderate evaporation.

jumbuck: a sheep.

squatter: in Australian usage a squatter was a member of the highest social class—the very wealthy pastoralists who were owners or lessees of vast tracts of land. The collective noun for these people, 'the squattocracy', gives a clear indication of where they stood politically and socially. Indeed, it was even seriously suggested (by one of their number) that they should form a House of Lords in Australia! At the time the song was written the squattocracy still exerted inordinate political power in the eastern colonies. (The Australian term 'selector' comes nearer to the standard English meaning of 'squatter'.)

tucker bag: a bag, often made of calico, which carried the bushman's food. Swagmen usually attached this bag to one of the swag straps.

'Waltzing Matilda' was written at a critical period in Australian history (although it might be argued that all of our history since the European invasion has consisted of crises of one kind or another). The 1880s had been a period of moderate harmony in industrial relations, as wool prices were high and the economies of the Australian colonies appeared to flourish. Spending in both the public and private sector was extremely high, but the money used had mostly been borrowed from the British. Then, in 1890, a financial collapse in Argentina led, in turn, to financial difficulties in London, which resulted in a withdrawal of funds from Australian banks. Numbers of banks were forced to close and a great deal of Australian industry ground to a halt. For the next three years (1890–93) the continent was in the grip of severe depression, and, among other problems, unemployment reached chronic proportions.

During the course of the preceding two decades, the bush workers had achieved remarkable progress socially, industrially, and culturally. They had begun to emerge as a highly distinctive group, with extremely advanced political ideas, strong social cohesiveness, a delight in intellectual and cultural pursuits, and a well-established code of ethics. Fundamental to the bushman's way of life was what was called 'mateship'; and it was this pervasive aspect of the bushman's philosophy which we find reflected in such things as his approach to unionism, his dreams of an ideal society, his reading, and his writing.

Because socialism and unionism were seen simply as extensions or the formalisation of mateship, Australia became by far the most highly unionised country in the world; and because the pursuit of knowledge and cultural enrichment were seen as infinitely superior to the pursuit of material wealth and comforts, the bush workers became the world's first truly literate—creatively literate—working class. And in their own special genre of poetry—the Bush Ballad—they developed the most distinctively Australian style of poetry. This was greatly encouraged by the birth, in 1880, of the journal that became known as the 'Bushman's Bible' and which spread its influence around the world: the Sydney *Bulletin*. Writing of those times, A. W. Jose records:

> A good deal of my time just then was spent up-country and I found everywhere men's—especially young men's—minds working as if some superbaker had permeated them with spiritual yeast . . . Never since [Elizabethan times] had a whole nation so unanimously clamoured for mind food.[1]

It was from this exciting intellectual and creative environment that a number of brilliant artists, draftsmen, prose-writers, and poets began to emerge as leaders in their respective fields. And as far as poetry was concerned, the writer who became by far the most popular was a young Bush Balladist who began writing under the pen-name 'The Banjo'.

Andrew Barton Paterson was born in 1864 at Narrambla, near Orange, New South Wales. His father was a squatter, and his mother also came from the wealthy landed class. However, Paterson's father lost a considerable amount of money in his attempt to acquire more land in Queensland, and he was forced to sell his station, Buckenbah, in order to cover his losses. A further bank loan enabled him to purchase Illalong Station, near Lambing Flat (now Young), but his purchase of this run coincided with the passing of the Land Acts which opened pastoral leaseholds to selectors. When these intending farmers began to select prime sections of the station, the bank foreclosed, and he lost Illalong too. However, the new owners allowed Paterson senior to stay on as manager, so the family were not made homeless by this further catastrophe. The future poet was about six years of age at this time, and these early experiences seem to have left an indelible impression on him.

Paterson attended Binalong public school in the heart of what had been, less than a decade earlier, country almost completely controlled by bushrangers, including the most remarkable gang of all—that founded by Frank Gardiner and taken through an extraordinary series of exploits by Ben Hall. Hall's first lieutenant, Johnny Gilbert, lies buried at Binalong, and Paterson attended school with the younger relatives—nephews and nieces—of several of the late members of this famous gang. It is interesting to observe, therefore, that in his early childhood Paterson had contact with both sides of the class struggle, and this was to influence his attitude throughout the remainder of his life.

Paterson did not stay long at Binalong School. His primary education was completed in Sydney, and he then attended, and matriculated from, Sydney Grammar School. From there he entered a lawyer's office and eventually he became a solicitor. When Paterson turned twenty-one in 1885, the *Bulletin* was about five years old, and it was towards the end of this year that Paterson decided to submit some of his writing to the already famous journal. He adopted the pseudonym 'The Banjo' after one of his father's thoroughbreds.

J. F. Archibald, the founder and editor of the *Bulletin*, was frank in his criticism of 'The Banjo's' verse, but encouraging—as this great litterateur always was when he recognised talent. In 1886 three of 'The Banjo's' ballads were published by the *Bulletin*, and from that time on Paterson went from strength to strength as a balladist. In 1890, 'The Banjo's' finest heroic ballad, 'The Man from Snowy River', appeared in the 'Bushman's Bible'; and by the middle of that decade, Paterson's poetry had become so popular that in October 1895 Angus and Robertson published a collection of his works under the title: *The Man from Snowy River and other verses*. It was an instant success and ran to reprint after reprint.

This collection was the first of ten books written by Paterson, the last one appearing in 1936, five years before he died. Some of these works were in prose; indeed Paterson as a prose writer is considerably underrated. But it was as a poet that he was loved by his compatriots, and so enthusiastic was his reading public that he became the second top-selling living poet: second only to Kipling, who, of course, had access to much greater markets than did 'The Banjo'.

Even though Paterson had settled more or less permanently in Sydney, he still retained his abiding interest in horses and his love of riding and other sports. Describing the poet, aged about thirty, Clement Semmler writes:

In Sydney Paterson had now become something of a social lion. It was not surprising. Well established in his profession; famous as a poet; a fine sportsman—tennis and polo player, horseman, huntsman, a first-class marksman—he had all the graces valued in the society about him. Added to this, he was a most handsome young man.[2]

In January of the same year that *The Man from Snowy River and other verses* was published (1895), Paterson went to Queensland for a holiday (and partly, also, on business in connection with his law firm). At the time, the young lion of Sydney was courting Miss Sarah Riley, whose family owned and lived on Vindex Station, about 35 kilometres south-east of Winton; and Paterson travelled the 1500 kilometres or so from Sydney to be with her. This holiday produced an important negative result, as far as the young couple were concerned, for the engagement was shortly afterwards broken off. But it also produced a very important positive effect, in that it was while on this holiday that Paterson wrote the words of 'Waltzing Matilda'.

The events leading up to the writing of 'Waltzing Matilda' are so interesting and have created so much controversy that a number of books and countless articles have been written about them. In fact it would be most surprising if there exists another single song about which so much has been written. In 1973, however, Richard Magoffin published the book which will almost certainly remain the definitive study, simply because, by dint of painstaking research, he has proven, once and for all, that the generally held belief regarding the song was quite correct. In addition, Magoffin has revealed a number of other aspects and details which not only support the accepted account, but provide further fascination to an already very interesting story. Other researchers such as Sydney May, who wrote the first book on 'Matilda' in 1944, and Harry Pearce, whose work appeared in 1971, also contributed substantially to our knowledge of the evolution of this remarkable song. Even the least reputable book on 'Matilda'—that by Oscar Mendelsohn—has played its part in piecing the story together. It so annoyed Magoffin by its incredible assertions that it moved him to pursue his own research with even greater energy and thoroughness. The following account draws material from various sources, but acknowledges by far its greatest debt to Richard Magoffin's excellent book: *Fair dinkum Matilda*.

The heroine of the Matilda story, quite by coincidence, appears in history as the baby who played a part in the violent demise of poor Dan Morgan—the slightly deranged bushranger who met his death on Peechelba Station, near the confluence of the Ovens and Murray rivers.

Morgan had crossed the Murray from his main haunts in the Riverina, apparently in response to the Victorian taunt that he wouldn't dare to do so. He bailed up Peechelba Station on the night of 8 April 1865, and proceeded, in his usual style, by gathering everybody into the homestead and whiling away the evening pleasantly enough with music and dancing.

In the morning, accompanied by the owner of Peechelba—Ewan Macpherson—he strolled down towards the horse yards in order to select a fresh horse from Macpherson's stable. But, unfortunately for Dan, he had unwisely allowed the nursemaid, Alice McDonald, to leave the main room (where the company were gathered) in order to attend to the Macpherson's baby daughter, Christina. And Alice did more than attend to baby Christina: she went to a neighbour's house and thereby got word to the police at Wangaratta. Thus, when Dan casually emerged from the homestead in the morning, it was, unknown to him, surrounded by troopers. Nevertheless, it was not the troopers who were responsible for his death, but a station hand called John Quinlan who had also been alerted and who stepped out from behind a tree and shot Morgan in the back.

Like many southern pastoralists, Ewan Macpherson was later to be greatly attracted to Queensland—just as Paterson's father had been—and as a result he purchased Dagworth Station, which is also near Winton but about 120 kilometres to the north-west of that town. Macpherson's sons went to Dagworth to run the property, while the rest of the family moved to Melbourne, and it was in that city that Christina Macpherson—the baby girl who had quite unknowingly contributed to Dan Morgan's capture—went to school and grew to womanhood. She was about the same age as the young poet whose works were becoming so popular through the pages of the Sydney *Bulletin*.

Christina Macpherson's younger sister, Margaret, married Stewart McArthur and lived on Meningoort Station near Camperdown, Victoria. And it was on this station that Christina spent many happy holidays as guest of her sister and brother-in-law. It so happened that she was at Meningoort in April 1894, and one of the highlights of her stay was the trip to Warrnambool, 70 kilometres away, to attend the celebrated annual race meeting which extended over three days: 24–26 April. (This was the type of meeting which governors attended, and which the stratum of society to which the Macphersons and McArthurs belonged attended picnics and balls as well as watching the actual races.)

The most interesting aspect of this particular meeting, from our point of view, was that one of the musical items performed by the Warrnambool Town Band at the races on both the 24th and the 26th was a march called 'Craigielee'. This march was by the migrant composer Thomas Bulch, who came to Australia in 1884 and who wrote under the name of 'Godfrey Parker'. It has long been a practice for composers to take simple song or dance tunes and to develop them into orchestral, piano, ensemble, or band pieces; and this is what Bulch had done on this occasion. The original music which he took as his inspiration was an old Scottish song tune called 'Thou Bonnie Wood o' Craigielea'.

None of this was of any concern to Christina Macpherson, but, being a musical person, she was quite captivated by that one particular tune, and, long after the Warrnambool race meeting was over, the tune of the 'Craigielee' march (or as near as she could remember it) kept coming back to her.

In December of that year (1894) Christina Macpherson's mother died, so Ewan Macpherson took his two unmarried daughters—Christina and Jean—to join his sons on the family property in Queensland.

Since the Macpherson station (Dagworth) was a short distance north-west of Winton, and the Riley property (Vindex) was an even shorter distance south-east of Winton, it should come as no surprise to learn that Sarah Riley and Christina Macpherson—who knew each other from their school days—should meet each other in the town. Sarah proudly introduced her handsome beau to Christina and her brother, Bob Macpherson; and 'The Banjo' and Sarah were invited to Dagworth for a stay on the Macpherson property.

Paterson was, indeed, delighted to go to Dagworth in order to see for himself the station, and particularly the remains of the woolshed which had been partially destroyed by fire the previous year.

Dagworth had been the scene of one of the most dramatic incidents in the great shearers' strikes which occurred more or less throughout the years 1891–94. This was a period of severe depression which followed the boom years of the 1880s. Squatters, such as the Macphersons, had decided to exploit the high unemployment by demanding what they called 'freedom of contract'—which really meant freedom for the squatters to name their own prices and their own conditions for the shearing of their sheep (the freedom of the shearers didn't enter into it at all!). Among other things the squatters began to lower the price being offered for shearing from £1 per hundred to 17s 6d per hundred—a substantial reduction.

By the 1890s, however, the old tradition of bush mateship had been transformed into highly organised unionism, and the shearers were not to be so easily deprived of their hard-earned pennies. They simply refused to shear on stations which would not pay the £1 per hundred. In retaliation the squatters imported hundreds of scab labourers, dredged from the large pools of unemployed in the southern cities, and refused to employ unionists. To make matters worse, the Government of Queensland, which was then entirely controlled by the wealthy land owners, used the military as well as the police troopers against the striking men. The only form of retaliation left open to the strikers then seemed to be to resort to the old 'swagman's friend'—their boxes of matches.

Shearing sheds went up in flames at various places throughout the vast sheep lands of Queensland and New South Wales, and six of the sheds to go were situated in the Winton district. It should not be imagined that the woolsheds on these great stations were something like an over-sized suburban backyard garage. Even a twelve-stand shed is a sizeable structure, capable of holding hundreds of sheep and with working space for various types of operation, including skirting the fleeces, classing, pressing, and so on—besides the actual shearing process. Some of these sheds had seventy or more shearer's stands—that is, they were huge outback factories in which, perhaps, 100 or more men would be employed, and were therefore worth a great deal of money.

Dagworth woolshed was a forty-stand shed—large by today's standards—and built to cater for the station's 80 000 head of sheep. Naturally the attack on it was not unexpected, especially after the neighbouring Ayrshire Downs shed had gone up in flames in July of 1894. The Macphersons had therefore taken the precaution of enlisting government help, and *three* troopers had been supplied (the number is significant in relation to our song). In addition, there were about seventeen other men under arms.

The attack finally came on the night of 1 September 1894. A small party of unionists crept to within 40 metres of the defenders, and, under a hail of gunfire from both sides, the shed was set alight. The shearers then withdrew, *apparently* without loss. The intense shooting prevented any attempt being made to save the shed, although it was not completely destroyed, and the Macphersons and their men probably felt quite relieved that they had all come through the ordeal unscathed.

On the following day a man named Samuel Hoffmeister was found shot dead in a union camp about 40 kilometres from the Dagworth head station. This seems to be an extraordinary coincidence, but his mates declared that he had committed suicide with his revolver, and the police could find no evidence to prove that this was incorrect. Neither were the police able to prosecute anyone for the incendiary attacks on the woolsheds.

All of this happened only a few months before 'The Banjo' arrived for his three-week stay on Dagworth in January 1895—and no doubt the whole district was still buzzing with the excitement of it when the poet was there.

Another interesting fact is that only a little over three years prior to Paterson's visit, a wool scourer named George Pope actually did drown himself by leaping (or falling) into the waterhole used for scouring on Dagworth. This incident occurred on 17 September 1891. Richard Magoffin further points out that a favourite picnic spot to which the Macphersons took Paterson, on at least one occasion, was Combo Waterhole which is situated in a beautiful billabong of the Diamantina River, near where Dagworth borders on Kyuna Station. In addition, according to Sydney May, on one occasion when Paterson was riding around the station with one of the Macpherson brothers they came upon the remains of a sheep's carcase which had obviously been butchered and partly removed—presumably by a passing swagman.

These several circumstances, combined with the interesting local term for carrying a swag, would have been more than enough to stir 'The Banjo's' poetic faculties. But what really set them going occurred one evening when Christina Macpherson played, on an autoharp, the catchy little tune she had heard at the Warrnambool races the previous April. Paterson was also captivated by the tune, and the result was 'Waltzing Matilda'.

It was a fair indication of things to come that the song proved to be immediately popular and was beginning to circulate in the Winton district within months of its composition. When it reached Hughenden (north-east of Winton), it created so much excitement that the whole town began to sing 'Waltzing Matilda'. Thus was born Australia's favourite song—and the story behind it is scarcely less remarkable than the song itself.

Some equally peculiar things were to happen subsequent to the composition of 'Matilda'. Firstly, Paterson never did marry Sarah Riley. John Manifold is of the opinion, with some justification, that there was a stormy altercation over the relationship which developed between 'The Banjo' and Christina Macpherson. Christina, incidentally, remained single until she died in 1935, but Paterson met Alice Walker of Tenterfield in 1902 and married her the following year.

Paterson quite rightly did not consider 'Waltzing Matilda' to be a true Bush Ballad, which is a form of poetry composed for *recitation*. 'Waltzing Matilda' is definitely a Bush Song and was composed to be *sung* to a specific tune. It therefore did not seem to belong in the collections of his work, such as *The Man from Snowy River and other verses*, which were collections of Bush Ballads for the spoken voice. Nor did it properly belong in another important collection which Paterson worked on for about a decade and published in 1905. This was his *Old Bush Songs*—which constituted the first major attempt to gather and preserve Australian traditional songs. 'Waltzing Matilda' could scarcely be classed as either 'old' or 'traditional' since he had only recently written it himself. Therefore the song remained unpublished for about eight years after its composition—although it was circulating quite widely in handwritten and oral forms. When it finally did reach the public in published form, it was in a rather odd way.

In 1903, Paterson sold the lyric of 'Waltzing Matilda' for a paltry sum to his publisher, Angus and Robertson, along with some other literary bits and pieces of what he termed 'old junk'. In the same year, Angus and Robertson sold the lyric to the firm of Inglis & Co, tea merchants. Inglis had decided to use the verses as an advertising gimmick for their proprietary line called 'Billy Tea'—by wrapping each packet of tea in a copy of the song. They obtained the words easily enough, but the music was not available, so Mrs Marie Cowan, wife of one of the firm's directors, was approached to arrange a musical accompaniment for the song. This she did, and it is indicative of the way in which 'Waltzing Matilda' had spread by this time that the tune in the piano accompaniment arranged by Marie Cowan in Sydney varies little from Christina Macpherson's original air. In fairness to Mrs Cowan it should be stated that she herself only ever claimed to have arranged the music for piano—not to have composed it. In its first publication in book form, 'Waltzing Matilda' appears in *The Australasian students' songbook* as an *arrangement* by Marie Cowan. It was not until 1917 that Paterson himself finally published the work, in the collection entitled *Saltbush Bill, J.P. and other verses*.

Paterson's understandable indecision about what to do with the song led to more unfortunate occurrences. Not long after he died in 1941 certain writers began questioning both the authenticity of Paterson's authorship and the authenticity of Marie Cowan's composition. Marie Cowan had never claimed to have done anything other than to arrange an existing tune (although her publishers had subsequently, of their own volition, changed the word 'arranged' to 'composed'), so the issue here is a fairly straightforward one. However, there have been attempts to show that the tune came from other sources than Christina Macpherson's moderately accurate recollections of the 'Craigielee' march. But arguments questioning Paterson's authorship have now been refuted beyond all doubt by the incontestable documentary evidence gathered and published by Magoffin in 1973. And Roger Covell, in his definitive work *Australia's music: themes of a new society*, has shown clearly that 'Craigielee' is not only the antecedent of 'Waltzing Matilda', it is also the parent tune of the best-known version of 'The Queensland Drover'.

One interesting development in recent years has been the popularisation of what is known variously as 'The Queensland version' or the 'Buderim tune' or the 'Cloncurry variant'. This is a version of 'Matilda' which uses an entirely different tune. The significant point is that this version incorporates Paterson's original lyric just as he wrote it, whereas the Cowan version (the best-known version of 'Waltzing Matilda') is a corruption of the original. This fact, and the fact that the Buderim tune has a more genuine 'folk' ring to it, has led serious students to the belief that this indeed was the *original* tune that Paterson heard when he composed the words; and that eventually both words and tune became corrupted by oral transmission to form the Cowan version with its unfortunate interpolations. Such, however, was not the case, and the most likely explanation is that, in the tradition of the bush, someone who hadn't heard of the Dagworth tune read 'Waltzing Matilda' when it was first published in book form in 1917, and decided to sing it: the Buderim tune was the result. It is, of course, a pity that the corrupted version of the lyric has become so well known, because, no matter which tune is used, Paterson's original words as printed in this book are distinctly superior.

Pro Hart, in this superb series of paintings, has been able to capture the true spirit of 'Waltzing Matilda'—the spirit in which it was originally written and the spirit with which it has been imbued by the people of Australia themselves. When Paterson heard troops singing it in camp prior to embarking for the battle front during the first World War, he said to Daryl Lindsay:

'Well, Daryl, I only got a fiver for the song, but it's worth a million to me to hear it sung like that!'[3]

One cannot help thinking that 'The Banjo' would also have been more than pleased by Pro Hart's interpretation of his most famous lyric.

REFERENCES
[1] Semmler, Clement. *A. B. (Banjo) Paterson*. Melbourne; 1965, page 15.
[2] Ibid, page 23.
[3] Semmler, Clement. *The Banjo of the bush*. Melbourne; Lansdowne, 1966, page 97.

Notes on each painting are by the artist

'In this painting I have depicted a typical swagman of the 1890s with his dog as his sole companion. The country is similar to that of the Menindee [New South Wales] district where I spent a great deal of time.'

49 cm x 46 cm, oil on hardboard

'This painting shows the loneliness of the swaggie's life. He has gone far enough for one day, and finding a suitable spot in the bush, he is getting a fire started so that he can boil his billy.'

46 cm x 31 cm, oil on canvasboard

'Most swaggies did not have tents, but when I was young I saw quite a few around the Menindee district using make-shift tents. The area is similar to Larloona Station, 110 kilometres south-east of Broken Hill, where I spent my childhood. I saw many swaggies pass through there during the Depression.'

46 cm x 61 cm, oil on hardboard

'A lone sheep wanders down to the billabong for a drink, and the swagman sees the opportunity for a good feed. In all my paintings I like to show an Australian atmosphere by combining different types of trees, so I have pictured the swaggie under trees incorporating features from the coolabah, box, and gum.'

46 cm x 61 cm, oil on hardboard

'The swagman grabs the jumbuck at the edge of the billabong. He probably has grabbed a few jumbucks before, and since the billabong is a fair distance from the station homestead he feels quite safe. Many station managers turned a blind eye to this sort of thing.'

46 cm x 61 cm, oil on hardboard

'After killing the sheep, the swagman helps himself to choice pieces of meat and stocks up his tucker-bag. Some swagmen put the wool back in place after they have removed the meat, thus making it look as if the sheep had died from natural causes. Here the swaggie's dog has also won a piece of the spoils.'

46 cm x 46 cm, oil on hardboard

'The crows are finishing off the carcass of the sheep. Often the swaggie would take only a portion of the meat and leave the rest to rot. During droughts on Larloona Station, I have even seen crows picking the eyes out of dying sheep.'

46 cm x 31 cm, oil on canvasboard

'The gentleman in blue is the irate squatter who has found the dead sheep on his station and summoned the police to investigate. They have caught up with the swagman and are challenging him to show them the contents of his tucker-bag.'

41 cm x 56 cm, oil on hardboard

'Here I have brought back into the painting all the elements of the swagman's dastardly act as he jumps into the billabong to avoid arrest. He commits suicide in the waterhole surrounded by coolabah trees.'

46 cm x 46 cm, oil on hardboard

'In this painting I have tried to get the feeling of the billabong haunted by the swagman's ghost. I wanted to show the feeling of eeriness that anyone might get when walking past such a place on a moonlit night.'

46 cm x 61 cm, oil on hardboard

'Morgan held the residents of Peechelba Station captive all night. I have visited the station and spent quite a bit of time studying the old furniture in the building to get the atmosphere for this painting. The scene is set in the dining room.'

46 cm x 61 cm, oil on hardboard

MORGAN AT PEECHELBA

'Christina Macpherson's nursemaid runs for help while Morgan holds up Peechelba Station. I have spent time at the station and am quite familiar with the area. However, the actual painting is not meant to be true to life but it aims to get across the atmosphere of the station in the 1860s.'

46 cm x 61 cm, oil on hardboard

"CHRISTINA MACPHERSONS NURSEMAID
RUNNING FOR HELP"

'Christina Macpherson hears the band playing "Craigielee" at the Warrnambool races. The scene is typical of a busy country race meeting. This is not an actual painting of the Warrnambool track; I got my inspiration from the local grandstand at Broken Hill.'

46 cm x 61 cm, oil on canvasboard

'This painting shows Banjo Paterson arriving at Dagworth Station. The buildings are not authentic for I wanted to give the feeling of the loneliness of the area and the bush at that time. The horses have wheels because they are only props for the historical subject.'

46 cm x 61 cm, oil on canvasboard

'I have depicted here the occasion when Bob Macpherson, Banjo Paterson, and a stockman discovered a dead sheep. After the swagman had enjoyed his feast, he left the remains under a tree.'

46 cm x 61 cm, oil on hardboard

'The Combo Waterhole was on the boundary of Dagworth Station and Kynuna Station, and it became a favourite picnic spot for people from both stations. The painting shows a picnic such as the one Paterson attended.'

46 cm x 61 cm, oil on hardboard

'Hughenden was apparently a very busy place around that period, with many coaches coming and going. Here again I have depicted the horses as toy ones which I believe gets the feeling of the subject across better than if I had painted real horses.'

46 cm x 61 cm, oil on hardboard

THE ROAD TO HUGHENDEN

'"Waltzing Matilda" was more or less launched at Hughenden. There was a big parade with much revelry, drinking, and firing shots into the air. The local paper printed the words on sheets that were pasted up on the walls of the hotels. The song was played by local bands and used in street marches.'

46 cm x 61 cm, oil on hardboard

'This painting depicts some Hughenden people enjoying a lively dance. It is the turn of the century and they are dancing to the tune of "Waltzing Matilda".'

35 cm x 27 cm, oil on hardboard

BIBLIOGRAPHY

Covell, Roger. *Australia's music: themes of a new society*. Melbourne, 1967.

Magoffin, Richard. *Fair dinkum Matilda*. Charters Towers, Qld, 1973.

Manifold, John. *Who wrote the ballads?* Sydney, 1964.

May, Sidney. *The story of "Waltzing Matilda"*. 2nd edn. Brisbane, 1955.

Mendelsohn, Oscar. *A waltz with Matilda*. Melbourne, 1966.

Pearce, Harry. *On the origins of Waltzing Matilda*. Melbourne, 1971.

Semmler, Clement. *A. B. (Banjo) Paterson*. Melbourne, 1965.

——. *The Banjo of the bush*. Melbourne, 1966.

Song Book Board of Sydney and Melbourne Universities. *Australasian students' songbook*. Melbourne, 1911.

Ward, Russel. *The Australian legend*. Melbourne, 1958.